MIKE MCCORMACK

The Magic of JOB MATCH

How to dramatically increase the performance of your organization

The Magic of Job Match

Copyright 2024 PeopleRight Consulting LLC, Mike McCormack.
All rights reserved.

ISBN: 979-8-9902805-0-2

Dedication

*This book is gratefully dedicated to the memory of Gordon K. Smith.
He was family, a friend, a confidant, a mentor, and a brilliant engineer,
and the time he spent with me had a huge impact
on how my life turned out.*

Table of Contents

Foreword vii

Acknowledgements xi

Introduction xiii

Chapter 1: Your Tests Become Your Testimony 1

Chapter 2: The Concept of Job Match 11

Chapter 3: What Your Employees Want 19

Chapter 4: Assessments 101 25

Chapter 5: Set Up for Success 35

Chapter 6: Predicting Future Performance (with Case Studies) . . 39

Chapter 7: Great Job Match Leads to Building Better Leaders . . . 53

Chapter 8: Moving Into the Future 59

Chapter 9: Afterwards: Taking the Next Step 65

About the Author 67

Foreword

Mark Twain famously said, "The two most important days in your life are the day you are born and the day you find out why." Mike authentically dedicates his life to helping individuals and teams discover the second part of Twain's story.

Mike McCormack endears friends quickly with a bigger-than-life curiosity and a penchant for adventure. Bringing intellect, early professional years in management consulting helping corporations overcome challenges, and the first-hand pain of being in a string of jobs that just didn't fit – all grant Mike a unique set of lenses with which to help identify patterns and clarify paths forward. Most importantly, helping individuals and organizations find the very best fit to unlock the wonderful human capabilities is Mike's life purpose.

Over more than a decade, I've witnessed Mike's love for helping people discover their capabilities, aptitudes, passions and calling - with relevant bearing in the ocean of data. Like a sea captain, Mike helps navigate statistical waves and norms, identifying where a person fits in the grand scheme of so many possible paths forward. The data is important because measurements in the abstract can often lead us astray.

Mike takes the data and the science of assessments seriously. And Mike often explains that this emphasis is important so that patterns and observations and recommendations for organizations and people be relevant to statistical norms. Measurements in light of benchmarks and proven patterns linked to performance offer a foundation solid enough for individual, team, and organizational fit. The navigator is wise who relies on a compass.

It's only fitting that a mutual management consulting professional and dear Christian friend, Jennifer Lewis Klouse, introduced us in late 2008. In fact, we all worked in the earliest stages of our careers at Andersen Consulting – one of the world's best management consulting firms. The common background afforded us first-hand knowledge behind the scenes, inside the senior leadership teams of the world's biggest and best companies.

We all shared a common set of observations we had seen in countless clients over the years. To riff on Jim Collins, we often saw too many people in the wrong seats on the bus. To be blunt, we all saw too many people in jobs that did not fit their knowledge, skills, and abilities. And we saw leadership teams skipping the fundamental step of creating an organization design that unlocks the most human potential.

We met together periodically to discuss the role of assessments and to understand the work Mike was doing with assessments and profiles and jobs and teams. We'd all become familiar with DISC, Myers-Briggs, StrengthsFinder, Enneagram, and so many other assessments. While some of these can be helpful, we were earnestly seeking the holy grails, the best assessments with statistical proofs, that could help find the ultimate job match or job-individual fitment. We discussed that assessments including or similar to Johnson O'Connor that focused on aptitudes and statistical norms going back to 1922 truly offered better science.

And yet, Johnson O'Connor was not an assessment that many companies or individuals could afford. And, even if they could, it wasn't the best assessment for organizational leaders as it does not profile the highest-performing people who currently occupy specific roles in specific organizations. Mike offered to share more about the assessments he had found success with and so our conversations included a healthy dose of strategy for the future, a better world for individuals, and relevant assessments and methodologies to serve leaders and their teams.

We all agreed with Mike that in this modern age, specialization continues to provide amazing advances in all fields, while simultaneously creating a problem of people knowing about all the nearly endless series of rabbit-hole specializations and then the added complexities of individuals finding their way to the best categories, let alone finding the best individual-job fit. And that's just the *individual* challenge.

The organizational challenge is equally daunting. How do organizations best identify the patterns of the high performers and then use those patterns to recruit, retain and provide ample career paths? Both parts of the puzzle offer great adventure for Mike who loves to craft better solutions to these challenges.

Over the years, I've been a consultant and client, having seen first-hand the great impact of Mike's assessments as we used them to profile top performers at my boutique consulting firm. I've been a fellow professional contemplating the amazing wonder of people and seeking to find the very best roles and jobs and career paths. And Mike and I and our families have become friends along the way. I am convinced that Mike McCormack is endeavoring to help solve one of the world's most challenging and rewarding puzzles.

The story deserves to be told and readers will gain valuable insights in the telling. Certainly, the reader can rest assured that Mike cares deeply about people and he offers predictability to a field once relegated to questionable methods. Mike brings years of experience and personal empathy and science to help organizations and individuals find a better path. Leaders will be equipped to better steward their most precious resources, their people. And Mike's faith adds texture and care – magnifying the recognition that the value of a person ignited in the right role is something wonderful beyond measure.

Scott Covington
Partner – Corporate Strategy, Mergers & Acquisitions
Credera

Acknowledgements

There are many people who helped me get where I am today, and none of them has had a bigger or more consistently positive impact on my life than my wife Vicki. Like any couple that has been married over 38 years, we have been over some mountains and through some valleys, and she has stayed strong by my side through it all.

I've dedicated this book to my lifelong friend, family member, and mentor Gordon K. Smith. Gordon was a brilliant engineer, and he had so many hobbies that it was hard to keep up with them all. He also was an avid reader and would regularly suggest books that I might like – on all kinds of diverse subjects. Gordon encouraged me to stick with my engineering major when I was contemplating changing my major in college. And it was Gordon who told me, "Mike, you don't have to be an engineer after you get an engineering degree, you can do anything you want."

Scott Covington has been a treasure that I have called on many times to strategize on how to build, promote, and grow a business that uses tools and processes that so few people (and companies) understand – to try and build the future that they truly want. He made himself available when I needed help, and when I hit the rough patches, and he has encouraged and inspired me for over 15 years.

I want to thank all the people who helped me learn this business, but especially Bernie O'Donnell, Brenda Daniel, Al Rainaldi, and Chris Kunze. Bernie and Brenda taught me this business, and basically took over my business for me when I was physically unable to run it (see chapter 1). Al shared a business model that has worked well in my business, and Chris showed me how important the data analysis phase can be in creating *predictive* results.

I also wish to thank the group of peers that I talk with every week by conference call who share ideas about what is working best, and how we can incorporate new ideas to better serve our clients: Greg Maciolek, Richard Stuckey, Wayne Outlaw, Tatyana St. Germain, Mike Kestly, and Lisa Hart Lowry. You continue to teach and inspire me every week.

Thanks to all the people who gave their time to read the initial draft of this book and added their thoughts, input, expertise, and suggestions, including past clients who have since retired: Randy Present and Bill Yancey, and long-time friends Wayne Lewis and Sandi Newman.

And I want to thank all the great clients with whom I have partnered these last 20+ years. Without your feedback, sharing what (and who) was working best, we could not have jointly built such high-performing teams.

Introduction

This book is for leaders, and one of the simplest ways to define a leader is that they are people with the ability to cause other people to follow them. More specifically, it is for leaders who recognize that the best way to reach their goals is to help the people on their team reach their goals.

To be clear, it is for leaders who realize that the only way they will succeed is if or when their team succeeds.

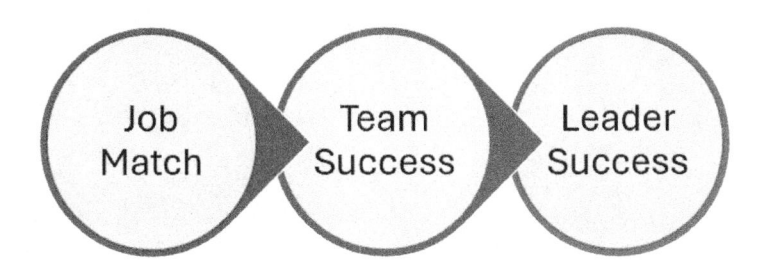

Job Match ▶ Team Success ▶ Leader Success

It has taken me a long time to complete this book. I started writing this book more than once but did not finish it because I wasn't sure of the best way to tell my story, and I wasn't sure I had accumulated enough *proof* to get my point across.

I apologize in advance if some of this material is too nerdy (i.e., detail oriented) for some of you. I've tried to explain everything, including how assessments work, in layman's terms as best I can.

I also apologize to those who want more details than what I have provided. My intent was to create a book that could be read on an airplane flight (or two), and then connect perhaps, and talk more later if you desire more detailed information.

After working with valued clients for over 20 years, including hundreds of leaders in all kinds of industries and roles, resulting in the development of hundreds of high-performer benchmarks, there is ample evidence that top performers are wired differently from all the rest. And I couldn't be more confident that what I write about in this book is true, and it is worth your time to find out why.

No matter what you have tried, or done, or read about in terms of improving the performance of yourself and your team(s), I challenge you to take a fresh look at what is described in this book.

To your success,
Mike

CHAPTER 1

Your Tests Become Your Testimony

Everyone has a story. And our stories determine who we become. So, to begin this book, I want to share two significant personal tests that meaningfully impacted my life and my career.

Test 1:

I never set out to have the career or business that I have now.

I went to college to get an engineering degree because I was good at math in high school. After receiving a civil engineering degree, I went to work in that field for a couple of years before I went back to graduate school to get a MBA, because engineering just didn't seem to be the right fit for me. I couldn't tell you why exactly, it just wasn't. And it wasn't because I couldn't do it, it was just that there was too much other stuff missing.

A more detailed view of my career path looks like this:

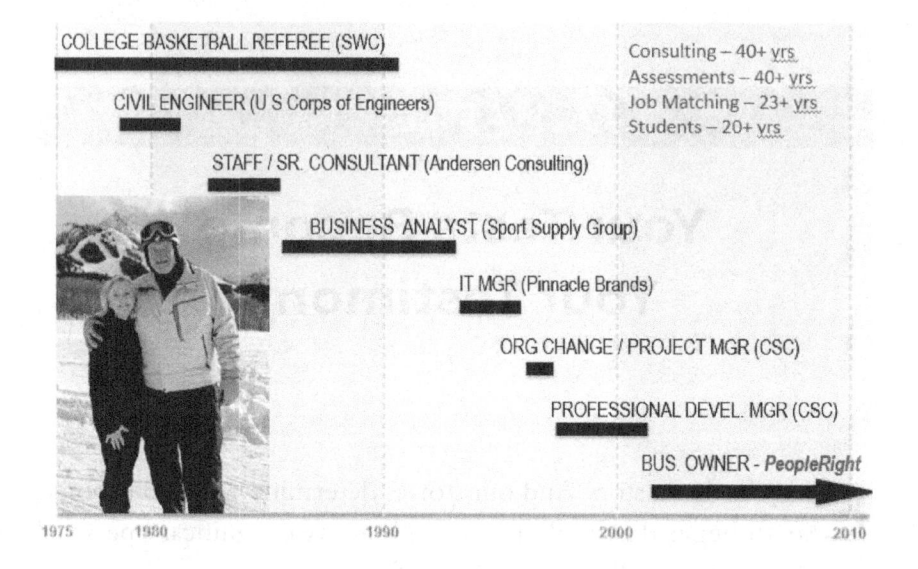

COLLEGE BASKETBALL REFEREE (SWC)	Consulting – 40+ yrs
CIVIL ENGINEER (U S Corps of Engineers)	Assessments – 40+ yrs
STAFF / SR. CONSULTANT (Andersen Consulting)	Job Matching – 23+ yrs
BUSINESS ANALYST (Sport Supply Group)	Students – 20+ yrs
IT MGR (Pinnacle Brands)	
ORG CHANGE / PROJECT MGR (CSC)	
PROFESSIONAL DEVEL. MGR (CSC)	
BUS. OWNER - *PeopleRight*	

1975   1980   1990   2000   2010

I include a picture with my wife Vicki (from a recent ski trip) because she has been with me throughout the entire journey, and there were many times and places where I could not have made it if it weren't for her love and support. More on that later in *Test 2*.

The short story of my 40-plus year career (to this point) is that during the first 21 years of my professional career I worked for five different companies and had 10 different job titles. I also had a somewhat strange hobby (basketball officiating) that I was pretty good at, and I rose to a level where I was officiating men's Division I college basketball games for a few years.

But of the 10 job titles I had, there were eight that I hoped I would never have to go back and do again, and there were two where I was in my *sweet spot*, where I was good at what I did, and I could do it well without having to get out of my comfort zone.

So, in the middle of my career, in my early 40s and married with two small children, I decided to start my own business. Perhaps I should say I was forced to start a new business. I had been a very successful consultant in an industry that the dot.com bust decimated, and I got laid off – so I *had to* do something new and different.

I considered my job history to that point, and thought, wouldn't it be great if I could use my engineering problem solving skills and my MBA to help companies make better people decisions that improve their bottom line. Help them get their employees into jobs where they could excel just by being themselves – and creating a true win-win scenario for both the employee and the employer.

I also want to clarify here that I have never had a job title that was in the Human Resources (HR) department of the business. I am not, nor have I ever been a recruiter or headhunter. But I wanted to improve the human experience and business results, and I wanted to find a way to provide information and processes that would help leaders who run the lines of business and HR professionals work together to make better people decisions.

I spent about 6 months planning how that might look, and then in early summer of 2001, I started PeopleRight. For those of you reading this who are good at connecting the dots, you may be thinking, wasn't that just before 9/11?

Well, yes, it was, and so the first few months were a very tough time for a new startup business. The whole world stopped, paused, and then reset after that fateful morning in our nation's history. Many businesses were hanging on for dear life, and few companies were willing to pay a startup company to help them do something they didn't believe was possible in the first place.

In a world where most small businesses fail in the first five years, PeopleRight has grown over the past 20+ years and partnered with some of the largest and most successful companies in the world. More on how we have done that later.

You might think our company's success was due to great goal setting, a solid business plan, and perseverance. Truth is, I grew up not being a very good goal-setter. You know, those people who set goals and then go out and accomplish them. Those kinds of people usually made me mad – mainly because I wasn't very good at it, or at least not very consistent about doing it.

I don't mean that I *never* set goals, I just didn't do it consistently. However, when I have set them, I have noticed that it tends to have a major impact on accomplishing those goals. Case in point: This book has taken over 13 years to complete…and I started two different times before, but never finished it.

On the few occasions that I *did* set goals, it proved amazing how well the results turned out. I can think of two specific examples of where I set a goal, and although I may not have been as diligent or consistent as I could or should have been in pursuing the steps to make them happen, I totally achieved the goals that I set. It is amazing how powerful our subconscious can be when we commit to something and allow our minds to inspire a path forward.

But yes, I did have a good business plan and lots of perseverance.

Test 2:

All of us think that we have it tough, and that some people just have an easy life. Truth is, all of us struggle, and everyone struggles in different ways. I like the coaching exercise that goes like this:

- In a group of people, ask everyone to sit in a circle with a pen and paper in their hand.
- Ask everyone to write on their piece of paper the three or four hardest things they are dealing with in their work, private, or family life, and then fold up the paper
- Pass a box around the room and ask everyone to put their paper in the box
- Take the box and shake it up, then pass it back around the room and ask everyone to take out just one piece of folded paper
- Most people, after reading what someone else is dealing with, would want their own piece of paper back!

In my case, the toughest thing I have ever had to deal with is a motorcycle wreck that happened in 2007, about one week after this picture was taken.

I set out on a beautiful Saturday morning from Dallas headed toward Glen Rose, TX – because there was a ride-friendly road (meaning it had lots of curves) between Granbury and Glen Rose that I wanted to enjoy.

Heading south-bound on FM 51 there is one 90-degree curve that was clearly marked with a large warning arrow, and I had slowed my speed accordingly (and I didn't think any more about that curve). When I reached the intersection of 51 and 67, I stopped and got off my bike and called Vicki. I told her it took me two hours to get down there, so I should be back home around noon.

Coming back north-bound, it turns out that same 90-degree turn was not marked with any kind of warning sign, and although I wasn't speeding, I was unable to keep my bike on the road. I left the pavement going between 40 and 50 MPH and rode the bike down into a gravel ditch that was a washed-out creek bed. Unable to regain control, I ditched the bike to my right and leaped off to the left. I landed face down in the gravel and it felt like my chest had collapsed and I could hardly breathe. It was the worst pain I have ever felt.

I don't know how long it took after I went down, but soon I heard voices from behind me, and they called for an ambulance. It seemed like a short time before the ambulance arrived (Glen Rose was about 15 miles away), and I could hear the sirens when it arrived. When I heard the ambulance driver approaching from behind, I heard him say very clearly to the people who had stopped to help me, "I'm not moving him, this is a *CARE-FLIGHT*."

The next thing I remember hearing was a helicopter landing nearby. Several people loaded my broken body onto a backboard, carried me to where the chopper had landed, slid me in, and strapped me down. I clearly remember the helicopter taking off, and looking out to see the rolling hills on the ground as it banked toward Ft. Worth, and then I blacked out.

Turns out that the wreck resulted in two cracked vertebrae in my back. I have two steel rods and 12 2 ½" screws holding my back in place today (see my x-ray below).

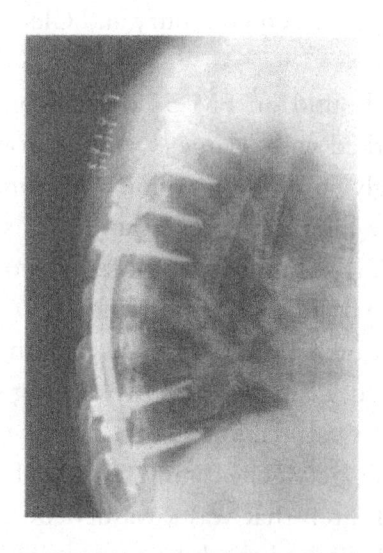

Additionally, I suffered two punctured lungs, cracked ribs, a concussion, a broken left wrist, and two badly injured shoulders. Think *Humpty Dumpty* after he fell off the wall.

Since the wreck occurred near Glen Rose, TX, I was flown to the nearest Level-1 trauma center, which was Ft. Worth's John Peter Smith Hospital (JPS). After two days I was transferred to Baylor Hospital near downtown Dallas. The fact that I got transferred to Dallas was a miracle in itself. I spent over five weeks unconscious in the Baylor intensive care unit (ICU) unit on a rotating bed while a large team of great doctors performed five major surgeries trying to piece my broken body back together again.

The best description of what my naked upper body looks like now is best described by a slogan I saw on a t-shirt: "*Scars are tattoos with better stories*". And I have at least 11 such *stories* resulting from my wreck. The three worst ones are the two where they had to force breathing tubes in between my ribs so that I could breathe while they were preparing me for all the five major surgeries they would perform while I was in the ICU, and the big *zipper* scar down my back where they put in the rods to stabilize my broken back.

A couple of weeks after the accident and while I was still in ICU, I developed a condition called *SIRS* (systemic inflammatory response syndrome), something where the key life-sustaining organs in your body start to shut down. The doctors told Vicki that they didn't know what caused this condition, and they didn't really know how to stop it. And if they couldn't stop it, I would likely die.

The primary doctor attending to me even suggested that Vicki bring the kids to see me – *if she wanted them to see me one last time!* For some *unexplained reason*, my symptoms slowly resolved, and my key organs started regaining their function. I learned from another doctor about a year after my wreck that patients over 35 years old rarely recover from *SIRS* – and I was 50 at the time of my accident!

After surviving SIRS and the five surgeries that were needed to put the big pieces of my body back together, I was transferred from ICU to the Baylor rehabilitation hospital. On the second or third day in rehab, the medical team performs an evaluation of your condition and outlines what they expect your recovery will likely be before you are released.

Vicki and I were told by my team of medical professionals that I would likely never walk again and may not be able to do many other daily tasks for myself either. I distinctly remember them using the term "he will be a total assist" several times, meaning that I wouldn't be able to do that type of activity ever again on my own! They said I would have up to 8 weeks in rehab, and then I would be going home (because insurance wouldn't cover a longer stay).

Around week two in the rehab hospital, they added aquatic physical therapy sessions to my daily routine. After a few short days in the pool my body started showing small signs of recovery, so they doubled my time in the pool. Trust me on this one – it is a lot harder to learn to walk the SECOND time, especially when you are 6'4", and the falls are a lot more painful, so the time in the pool helped on a lot of fronts.

The pain in my back was excruciating, but at least I was slowly becoming mobile again. After the fifth week in rehab, I was doing well enough to take a small excursion for a few hours outside the hospital, and I asked if we could go to church. I not only wanted it for me, but to show all the people who were praying for me that their prayers were having a positive impact on my recovery.

After six and a half long weeks in the rehab hospital (and one week earlier than expected) I was discharged to go home, and I got to sleep in my own bed for the first time in nearly three months. All the physical therapists in the rehab hospital who worked with me said that I was a walking miracle when I left.

I didn't try to start working again until I had been home for a few months, and it was very slow in the beginning. It was several months after I came home before I was able to drive a car, and every tiny bump that I hit sent huge waves of pain down my back. I went to a 'pain management doctor' for medications to ease the pain, and he swore that he was prescribing dosages that would 'put down a horse', but they didn't seem to help relieve my back pain much.

It took over a year before I was back into a full work schedule. If people who didn't know I had been in a wreck saw me, most of them couldn't tell anything had happened (unless we were playing golf – and the rods in my back made my golf game really bad).

Fast forward to today, and after not going snow skiing (the slopes are my true *happy place*) for 13 years after my wreck, I have now gone skiing six times in the last four years.

Which leads to the *testimony*.

So, what do my two *test* stories above have to do with this book?

Jeff Burnett, a long-time friend of mine and retired pastor, shared this quote with me: **"I am immortal until the will of God for me is accomplished."** – David Livingstone

The fact that I am still here after my wreck is proof that God isn't done with me yet. It wasn't until recently that I realized the connection between my two biggest life tests, and that I needed to finish this book.

The two tests I have been through (my career path and my accident) show that there are a lot of things that happen to us in life that we cannot predict or prevent, and we just must learn to deal with them. And it is true that bad things can happen to good people.

But there are also a lot of other things in life that we *can* predict with accuracy, like how well someone will fit in a job, and therefore how well they will perform, and that's what the rest of this book is about.

We'll start with defining what drives job performance.

CHAPTER 2

The Concept of Job Match

If you have ever had a job that was in your sweet spot, you will relate well to this chapter. Any job where you are a perfect fit makes it easy to be successful, and success drives performance, and performance drives longevity, and things just don't get much better.

In previous generations, many people never experienced a great job fit because people just didn't have that many jobs. If the first one or two you chose weren't a good fit, you were basically stuck. In my parents' generation, for example, if a person had more than two or three jobs, they were often thought of as unstable or unreliable – because 'good people' just didn't change jobs often. And people stayed with a company much longer than they do today, often all the way to retirement.

Today, most people have had more than seven jobs before they turn 30! According to data from the U.S. Bureau of Labor Statistics (BLS), the average number of jobs held by individuals ages 18 to 28 is 7.2. This data indicates that young adults often experience multiple job changes in the early stages of their career.

Having the ability to work in multiple jobs lets people experience how much job fit impacts their success, satisfaction, and longevity in a job.

As I explained earlier, I had 10 different job titles, with five different companies, and in three different industries before I turned

40. In retrospect, part of me believes I was fortunate to have those experiences because there were two jobs that were head and shoulders above the rest in terms of job fit for me. I loved both of those roles, I was a top performer, and I made more money! I had less stress at work (and at home), I had more fun, and people around me knew I was in my sweet spot.

People who have experienced great job match want to feel that satisfaction repeatedly. People who haven't experienced it wonder if it exists.

According to *Harvard Business Review*, the "job matching" approach more accurately predicts job success than any of the commonly accepted factors, such as education, experience, or job training. A study that followed 360,000 people through their careers during a period of 20 years demonstrated that a key ingredient in retaining people is ensuring that they are matched to their jobs in terms of their *abilities, interests, and personalities*.

To illustrate these three different types of traits, think about the things you consider when you buy a new vehicle:

1. Engine/Power plant (can it do what you want/need it to do?)
2. Interior (for comfort or "fit")
3. Accessories (some of which you won't understand or may never use)

And when you use a ***whole-person*** assessment, it is very similar:

1. Cognitive traits – Can they process information well enough to do the job?
2. Behavioral traits – How will they "fit" with others doing this job, with clients, and with you?
3. Interests – Knowing these can be helpful in some ways, but *usually not very predictive of performance*

Only about 10 percent of a person can be observed on the surface. Ninety percent of a person's potential lies below the surface. I like to think of it like the iceberg analogy. There is a large percentage of a person that can be under the surface, including things like learning style, behavioral tendencies, and occupational interests.

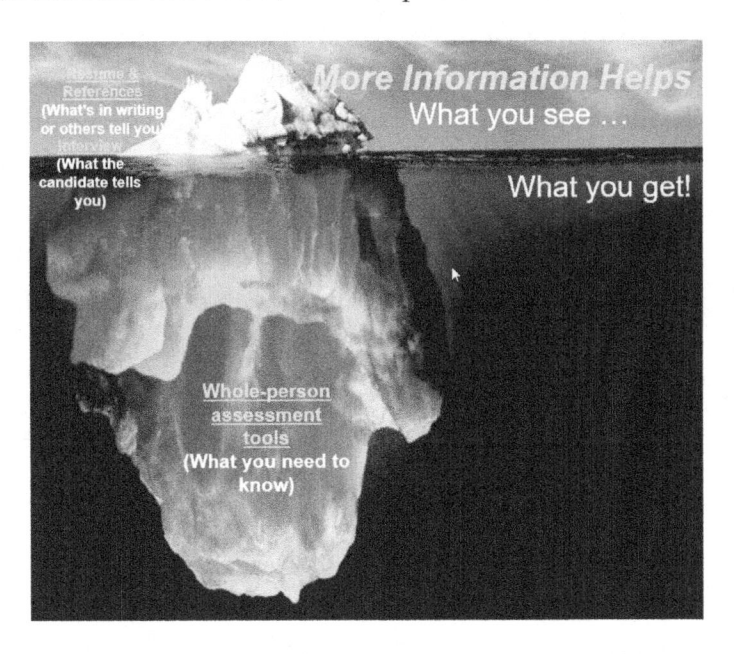

The study found that when you put people in jobs where the demands of the job matched their abilities, where the stimulation offered by the job matched their interests, and where the cultural demands of the position matched their personalities, staff turnover decreased dramatically, and *productivity increased drastically*.

Job match is critically important in predicting job success, but there are also types of fit that can also be important, including:

- A work environment where they can thrive – the impact of work environment has changed dramatically since the Covid outbreak in 2020. Jobs that were once considered to be in the office only became 'work from home' jobs almost overnight, and when people (and some companies) saw they could be just as productive from home as from the office, many never went back. Or they went back into the office on some type of hybrid schedule.

- Organizational culture can also have a huge impact on job success. How an organization treats its employees, or what causes they promote (or tear down), and how conservative or liberal the leaders are can drive people *to* or *from* organizations.

- How they fit in with other team members can be a huge factor also. How likely are they to get along with the team, can they keep pace with others who are succeeding in the role, or can they learn quickly enough to keep up to date in their industry.

- One of the biggest drivers of how well people fit into their job is how they fit in with their boss. Some studies show this factor causes more people to leave their job than how much money they make. There can be some overlaps here between some of the other job fit categories already described, but it really deserves separate consideration.

Job success can be influenced or enhanced by all kinds of other individual factors, including:

1. Hard Work and Dedication - Putting in the effort and time required to excel in your role can greatly contribute to success. Being committed to doing your best work consistently is essential.

2. Skills and Knowledge - Possessing the necessary skills and knowledge relevant to your job function is crucial. Continuously improving and staying updated on industry trends helps individuals stay vital and competitive.

3. Effective Communications - Being able to communicate clearly and effectively with peers, clients, and superiors is essential for collaboration, problem-solving, and achieving goals. It is difficult to promote someone to a leadership position if they haven't mastered the use of proper grammar and have developed effective business writing skills.

4. Adaptability - The ability to adapt to changing circumstances, learn new tasks, and navigate challenges is key in a dynamic work environment.

5. Teamwork - Collaboration and the ability to work well with others leads to greater productivity, innovation, and success in achieving personal and professional goals.

6. Problem-solving – The ability to identify issues, analyze them, and come up with effective solutions is a valuable skill in any job.

7. Leadership – Taking initiative, demonstrating leadership qualities, and inspiring others contributes to individual and team success.

8. Time Management – Effectively managing your time and prioritizing tasks can help you stay organized, meet deadlines, and accomplish goals efficiently.

9. Positive Attitude – Maintaining a positive attitude, even in challenging times, can foster resilience, creativity, and a more productive work environment.
10. Networking – Building relationships within your industry and expanding your professional network creates opportunities for career advancement and success.

But even if a person excels in all of these areas, if they are not a good fit for the job in terms of cognitive skills, personality, and interests, it likely will not turn out well.

Job match is achieved when an individual's skills, abilities, interests, and values align with the requirements and characterisitics of a particular job or role within an organization. The impact of job match on job success is significant and influences various aspects of an individual's performance and job satisfaction.

When a person's skills and abilities closely match the demands of the job, they are more likely to perform well. They can quickly adapt to the tasks and responsibilities, leading to higher productivity and efficiency.

Good job fit also enhances job satisfaction because people feel a sense of fulfillment and accomplishment when their work aligns with their interests and values. Alignment here also reduces stress and frustration associated with mismatched job demands.

Employees who experience a good fit between themselves and their job generally tend to be more engaged in their work. They are more committed to the organization's goals, more entusiastic about their tasks, and more willing to invest discretionary effort.

Good job fit can play a crucial role in employee retention. When people feel that their skills and and interests are valued and utilized effectively in their role, they are more likely to stay with the organization for the long term. Conversely, mismatches in job fit can lead to more turnover as employees seek opportunities that align better with their skills and preferences.

Ensuring job fit across the organization can contribute to overall organizational performance. When employees are well-suited to their roles, they can collectively drive efficiency, innovation, and customer satisfaction, which ultimately leads to increased success of the organization.

And job fit can have a positive influence on career development opportunities. Employees who are in roles that align with their strengths are more likely to seek out and excel in advancement opportunities in the organization.

Overall, the impact of job fit on job success underscores the importance of assessing individual capabilities and preferences when making hiring decisions and designing new roles within an organization. Striving to achieve optimal job fit can lead to improved performance, satisfaction, and retention for both employees and employers.

At the danger of over-simplifying things, think of it this way:

- Job match drives job performance
- Job performance drives job success
- When the people on your team succeed, *you* succeed!

Still not convinced how important job match can be? In the Sept 1998, Vol 124, No. 2, pp 262-274 of *Psychological Bulletin,* there was an article titled "The validity and utility of selection methods in personal psychology: Practical and theoretical implications of 85 years of research findings", where they measured the relative outputs of superior, average, and 'non-producer' workers in three separate levels in an organization:

Unskilled / Semi-skilled

- 'Average' workers output = 19% more than 'Non-producers'
- 'Superior' workers output = 19% more than '*Average*'
- 'Superior' workers output = 38% more than Non-producers'

Skilled

- 'Average' workers output = 32% more than 'Non-producers'
- 'Superior' workers output = 32% more than '*Average*'
- 'Superior' workers output = 64% more than Non-producers'

Management / Professional

- 'Average' workers output = 48% more than 'Non-producers'
- 'Superior' workers output = 48% more than '*Average*'
- 'Superior' workers output = 96% more than 'Non-producers'

To summarize the data above, it says that the difference between a top and bottom producing management professional in your organization is that the top producer will have an output nearly twice as much (96% more) than a bottom producer. And the higher the role is in the organization, the bigger the difference in performance will be.

Quoting more recent data that further emphasizes this point, McKinsey and Company completed a study in 2023 (*The State of Organizations 2023*) stating that between 20 and 30 percent of critical roles *aren't* filled by the most appropriate people, and **the highest performers are 800% more productive than average performers.**

Up next is what your employees want out of their work – because leaders need to know what their people want and expect.

CHAPTER 3

What Your Employees Want

Last year I personally conducted online research about what employees want most from their employers. I started by compiling a list of 50 things that people want most, and then put those things into categories (or similar themes) and then looked at the top four categories.

- Great Job Match
- Competitive Compensation
- Career Growth Opportunities
- Great Coaching

Job Match

It shouldn't come as a surprise that ***job match*** was #1 because of all the things we covered in the last chapter. And the other top three categories shouldn't come as a surprise either, but it helps to point them out because they are what your employees want and expect. Remember, employment is a two-way street, and it must work for *both* parties!

Again, and not to oversimplify, but another way to think about job match is: Can the person be successful in the job just by being themselves, not having to constantly get out of their comfort zone to get things done that are required by this job. It can certainly require some specific knowledge and experience in many cases, but it makes everything work better when it is present.

Competitive Compensation

Competitive compensation (or the lack thereof) is often thought of as the primary reason why most people leave jobs. And while it is an important factor in the overall employee experience, in most cases it is not *the most i*mportant factor. In cases where it is not the most important factor, the most important factor is typically the employee's relationship with their boss.

I've known Brad Smith, an Executive Coach in the Dallas – Ft Worth area for a long time, and Brad sends out regular quips and quotes, one of which is included below:

> "The most important thing in your career isn't:
> - *Your fancy office*
> - *The amount of money you earn*
> - *Your job title*
>
> It's the leader you report to. If the leader you work with sucks, your job will be a nightmare.

Be fussy about who you work for. Find someone who will give you the luxury of looking forward to Monday."

I asked some of my key clients to review this book prior to publishing it, and one of them shared with me the two best jobs they ever had were when they were working for great leaders (not when they were making the most money). And they defined great leaders as people who really cared about their people and provided a safe environment for them to grow as a new leader.

Compensation is important, and it is determined by multiple factors, and oftentimes many different people have an input into compensation within an organization. And don't forget, there are lots of online resources where your employees can find out what their peers in other companies and industries are making.

Career Growth Opportunities

The importance of career growth opportunities for employees is becoming increasingly important, especially for younger workers. Since there is no longer any stigma attached to listing many different jobs on your resume like in the past, your employees know they can try something else if what they are doing now isn't working out for them. And in most cases, they can try other jobs out for other employers just as easily as they can try them out for your company. And if that doesn't work out, they'll just try again. Since they all grew up in the video game era, think of it as them having the 'game reset' mentality, i.e., if they feel they are in a 'losing situation', they will just hit the reset button and start over!

What if you took job match seriously in your company, and you measured the key traits and characteristics of the people who performed best in any given role, and you could create benchmarks showing what all these people have in common? And what if you could compare any future candidate's characteristics to these benchmarks to see how similar they are to your best performing people in this role?

Consider what every college and pro sports team does to build their rosters. They compile data about their most successful athletes at every position, and they use that data to analyze any future additions to their roster. And while it is never an *exact* science (although no one wants a running back or defensive back who can't run a sub-5.0 second 40-yard dash), it certainly works better than *no* science, and the more data they have accumulated and analyzed the more accurate their future choices become. I know people on college and pro personnel staff, and they are on teams of more than *20 people* who are all constantly evaluating job fit and how to add new (and better) talent to their organizations.

Getting back to your own company's situation, think of compiling job match data for *ALL* the key jobs in your company. If you collect specific data about a candidate's skills, behaviors, and interests before they are hired for their first job in your company, you can use that same information later to see how they compare to other key jobs, and you can help them develop plans for how to prepare for the next job while they are still in their current position.

Great Coaching

Coaching may have some overlaps with the other three areas, but it can be a differentiator on its own. What many people fail to realize is that great coaching always begins with a thorough understanding of yourself as the coach (more on this later), and then an understanding of your pupil, or employee.

You may or may not realize this, but we all think that we are 'normal', and when people are different from us, we think they are 'abnormal', or messed up, or screwed up, or some other derogatory term.

But it's not that they are messed up, or screwed up, or whatever, it is just that they are wired differently than you, and different can sometimes be good and sometimes be bad, depending on a lot of factors. Things like what kind of work you are asking them to do, and who they will be working with, for, and around.

In addition to knowing how a potential hire compares to you as their leader, how great would it be if you also knew how they compare to your best people? What if you could coach in a very targeted manner, focused on a person's specific strengths and weaknesses, rather than putting everyone through the same training?

And as they get ready to move from being one of the team to a leader of a team, what if you could show them how others will likely see them as a leader, based on how they are wired compared to how everyone else is wired?

Coaching employees is something that is always resource constrained. Just think about how much ahead of the competition you would be if you could develop a personalized development plan for each person based on information that you can collect before they ever start working at your company.

Next, we will talk about how assessments work; stuff that most people don't know or understand.

CHAPTER 4

Assessments 101

Today it's hard to meet someone who has never taken some kind of assessment, or who doesn't think they know all there is to know about assessments, or who doesn't think that all assessments are the same. But most people know very little about assessments or how they work, what they measure, how well they measure it, or how applicable the scores are for predicting future performance.

Many Different Types

When you use the word 'assessment', most people think you are referring to one of the thousands of different ***personality-style tools***, because they are the most prevalent assessment used today. There are no 'right' or 'wrong' answers on these types of assessments, and they usually take 20 – 30 minutes to complete, so people are generally agreeable to taking them.

Almost all personality-style tools are based on some type of four-quadrant matrix that is determined by assigning scores to two primary axes. The axes that are used most frequently on these assessments are *Task focused* Vs. *People focused* and *Introvert* Vs. *Extrovert*.

The results from these two scales define which quadrant a person falls into, and from there the assessment provider usually makes lots of predictions about a person's personality and communication style based on that information.

Many of these tools are referred to as DISC tools, of which there are hundreds of different versions, and they have a model similar to the one shown below.

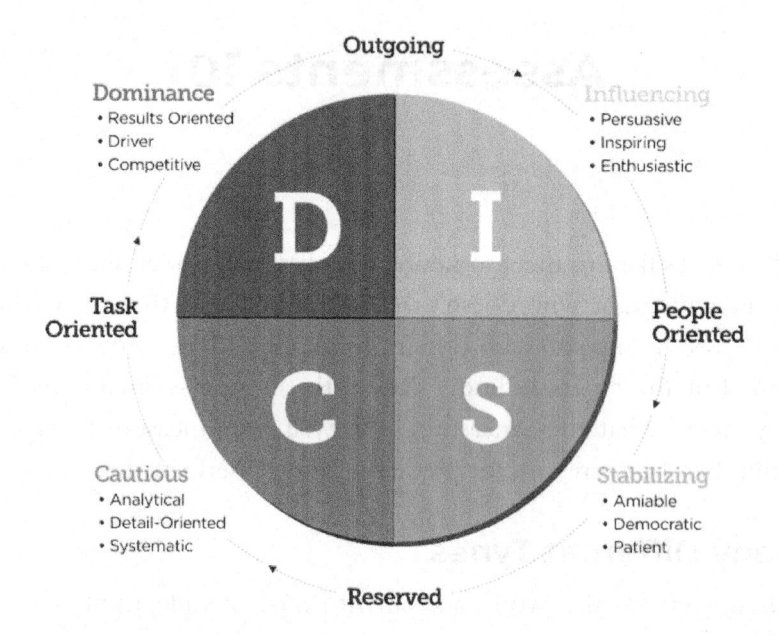

Outgoing

Dominance
- Results Oriented
- Driver
- Competitive

Influencing
- Persuasive
- Inspiring
- Enthusiastic

Task Oriented

People Oriented

Cautious
- Analytical
- Detail-Oriented
- Systematic

Stabilizing
- Amiable
- Democratic
- Patient

Reserved

Another type of assessment is one that measures **skills or abilities**. On these assessments there is always a 'right' (or 'wrong) answer, and scores reflect how many questions the candidate got 'right'. They usually measure, at the very least, math and verbal skills, and can also measure other types of skills and abilities. These are usually much more reliable (defined below), but they usually take longer to complete. ACT and SAT exams fall into this category when they are measuring math and verbal skills.

Another type of assessment is the **interest inventories**. Interest inventories have nearly become an industry unto themselves. And while they may be helpful in some ways, they aren't likely to accurately predict (used in isolation) how well someone will perform in a particular job.

Think of it this way: I may love doing something but be terrible at it, or I may hate doing something but be good at it. The value of interest inventories is that they can be a predictor of how long someone will stick to it, because we will continue to do things we love even if we aren't very good at it.

Whole-Person Assessments

When you combine all three of the types above, we refer to that as a *whole-person* assessment, because it is not focusing on just one area but on all three separate areas of how a person is wired. The whole-person assessment that we normally use measures 20 separate traits related to cognitive skills, personality, and interests. One way to think about it is like a Swiss Army knife – because you can do so many different things with the assessment results.

U. S. Department of Labor (DOL) Guidelines

I must include in this section what is recommended – because not all businesses who use assessments know this information or follow what is recommended. The **U.S. Department of Labor** published guidelines in 1999 that were 97 pages long and were summarized in the last chapter into 13 key points.

1. Use assessments in a purposeful manner
2. Use the *whole person* approach
3. Make sure the instrument is unbiased and fair
4. Use *reliable* instruments
5. Make sure it is *valid*
6. Use assessment tools that are appropriate for the target population.
7. Use assessment instruments with understandable & comprehensive **documentation available**
8. Ensure that administration staff are properly trained
9. Ensure that testing conditions are suitable for all test takers
10. Provide reasonable accommodations in the assessment process for people with disabilities
11. Maintain instrument security
12. Maintain confidentiality of assessment results
13. Ensure that scores are interpreted properly

About nine or ten of those 13 guidelines are easily met by most assessment tools, but the other three or four guidelines separate the winners from the losers – especially when they are used for predicting job match.

The first one of these differentiating guidelines is #1 on the list – companies should <u>only use tools that are designed for the specific purpose that they are being used</u>. This sounds straight forward enough, but you would be surprised at how many businesses use four quadrant personality-type tools such as MBTI and Disc-type tools, which are designed as communications style or team-building tools - in the employee selection process (where they are ***not*** recommended for use).

And if you are wondering why these types of tools aren't recommended for use in selection decisions, it is usually because of reliability and validity.

Reliable Vs. Valid

The second recommended criterion that is often broken or ignored is #4: Companies should not use any tool for job selection that is not reliable, (i.e., that produces inconsistent results when it is taken multiple times). If you get different results every time you take it, it shouldn't be used in making employee (hiring) decisions. If the tool is not recommended for use in hiring decisions, I don't know why anyone would want to use it for career coaching or strategic career planning decisions.

This may be more information than you want to know, but the DOL document referenced above suggested that only assessments that achieved *reliability scores greater than or equal to 0.80 should be considered 'Good'*, and those with *scores below 0.70 may have 'limited applicability'*. You would be surprised (shocked maybe) to see how some of the most popular personality-style tools and interest inventories compare against these criteria. (The *average reliability score for the tool we use with our clients is over 0.80*, and all the personality characteristics we measure have reliability scores above 0.78)

The third differentiator is that companies should only use tools in the hiring process if they are *valid* (number 5 above) – **meaning one can demonstrate that results from the assessment can be shown to correlate to performance on the job**. The DOL document states that reliability coefficients should be above 0.35 to be 'very beneficial', and between 0.21 and 0.35 to be 'useful'. Again, the tool we use with our clients falls into these higher ranges.

If an assessment doesn't pass the **reliability** test it cannot be a **valid** instrument. And just because it is **reliable** does not necessarily mean that it is **valid**.

Let me give you an example. A tape measure would be a *reliable* instrument for measuring an individual's height, and assuming they were full grown, height doesn't change much after humans become adults, so this would be a *reliable* tool for measuring height. But if I used a person's height as a criterion for job selection, it would fail the *validity* test in almost all cases because a person's height does not impact their ability to perform in 99.9% of the jobs out there.

The more you know about assessment tools the less likely that you will be disappointed in the results from these tools. And remember, it's not just the toolset, but understanding how to use and apply the information to your current situation (number 8 above).

Distortion

Another key trait for any assessment instrument is whether it is capable of measuring distortion. Distortion is defined by how candid or frank the respondent was while taking the assessment. In some cases, like when measuring cognitive skills, distortion is irrelevant because they either got it right or they got it wrong.

In cases where assessments measure personality or behavioral traits it can be vitally important because you need to know how likely it is that the scores are truly indicative of who this person really is.

Distortion relates to the reliability of the results, not the honesty of the individual. And it can happen because of an attempt to portray a picture of how they would like to be seen versus how they are wired.

So, before you use any assessment results in your people decision-making processes, you should know if there is any distortion in the results you are using.

How Assessments Are Scored

What if you used a tool that measured how much of a specific trait someone has, as compared to how much of that trait that other people have? We call this a **normed** assessment. Think of the 10–point scale with a bell-shaped curve over it, and where most people's scores fall down the middle of the curve (between 4 and 7), and some people fall to the left (between 1 and 3) and some to the right (or between 8 and 10).

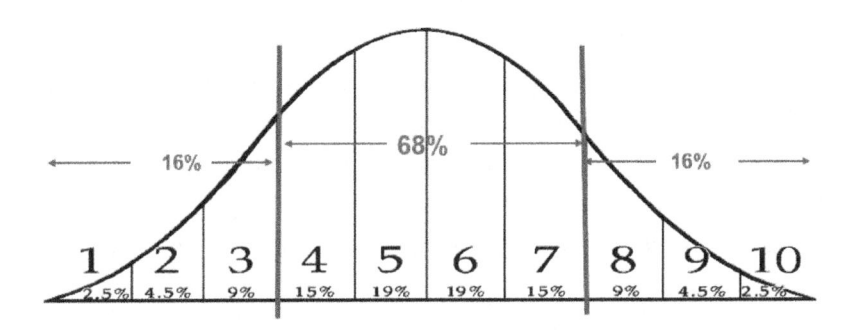

This graph illustrates that if someone scores a 1 or a 10 on a standard 10-scale scoring system that only 2.5% of the population will score a as they do. Said in a different way, they are different than 97.5 % of the population. Having more or less of something than 97.5% of the population means they are unique in this trait, and even if they don't realize it, most people around them will likely notice how *unique* they are.

There can be both advantages and disadvantages to having more or less of a certain trait than everyone else. And it depends on what role someone is being asked to play, and the people they are working with, for, and around.

When we know this information about ourselves (i.e., where we score compared to everyone else), AND about all the people who work for us, just think about how much better of a coach you could be. If we know what our core skills and behaviors are, and what our subordinates core skills and behaviors are, we could understand that just because they are different from us doesn't mean that they are *bad* people, it just means they are *different*.

Allow me to share a couple of examples.

What if you could measure how trusting or optimistic people are? People who score low on this scale (1- 3) are people who tend to be much less trusting and optimistic than people who score high (8 – 10) on this scale. If I have a Controller in my business, I may hope they score low on this scale, because a low score suggests that they don't trend to trust people, and therefore they typically ask a lot of questions before they start to feel comfortable that the information they have been given is correct.

They may ask four to six questions before they start to feel comfortable with the numbers that someone else gives them, which only increases the odds that the numbers are, in fact, accurate or reliable. If they didn't ask these questions, and the information that they were given was not accurate and they accepted it anyway, and put it into the financial statements, then every number that follows would be inaccurate because it was based on faulty information.

What if we could measure how people prefer to make their decisions, with the scores of 1 – 3 indicating someone prefers to use their intuition or gut feel to make decisions, and scores of 8 – 10 are reflected by people who make their decisions based solely on facts, data, or logic. Neither way of making decisions is *always* right or wrong, but it can result in some interesting situations and outcomes.

Years ago, I was on the board of a small private school, and we had board meetings once a month. We always hoped that these meetings would take only one or two hours, but they usually took three to four hours. And they often included many contentious discussions along the way. Toward the end of my term on the board I recommended that our entire board complete an assessment, and how people make decisions was one of the many traits that it measured.

It turns out that half of our board members were making their decisions on the tough issues we were facing based largely on their gut feel, and the other half were making their decisions on facts, data, and logic. So, half the board could never understand how the other half could possibly make the decision they were making, which led to some very unproductive arguments, bad feelings among the members, and extremely long meetings. If we could have just realized how people were making their decisions, we could have had much more productive discussions and come to agreements on issues much faster.

Now think about having nineteen additional traits that are proven to have an impact on job performance, and we could measure all twenty of them accurately, how beneficial that would be!

Normed Vs. Ipsative

The other type of scoring on assessments (than **normed**) is called **ipsative**. Most of the personality-style tool assessments fall into this category. The way these tools work is that they ask you to describe yourself, and then they report back to you what you told them about yourself.

You may think of yourself as outgoing because the people you typically hang around are less outgoing than you are, but compared to the working population you aren't more outgoing than most. Your perspective is limited to those you compare yourself to, so the results can be limited by your own perspective.

This approach is as old as time, and even mentioned (but not favorably) in the Bible, where in 2 Cor 10:12 it says, "…but when they measure themselves by themselves, and compare themselves with themselves, they are without understanding." (*New American Standard version*).

I always smile when people say that they took an assessment and the results really 'nailed them'. Well, if it was an **ipsative** assessment, that is how it is designed to work – to report back to you exactly what you think about yourself and what you told it – regardless of how accurate your view of yourself may be.

Now that you understand how assessments work, we can cut to the chase - and show how job match can enhance leaders' ability to predict future performance.

CHAPTER 5

Set Up for Success

Now that we have covered how properly designed assessments work, it is time to start talking about how to use them to make better people decisions that will improve the performance of your team. The best place to start when you want to improve job performance in your company is by better understanding yourself, and how you are wired.

After over twenty years in this business, I'll share that we will NOT work with any new client company if their leadership team won't do this self-evaluation step themselves and go through a personal feedback review session with me before they ever try to understand how to use this information with other people.

I learned this lesson working with clients who were looking to improve the leadership scores of their leadership team (which is a topic that deserves a book of its own), and I learned that if the leader at the top of the organization wasn't willing to go through the leadership development exercise for themselves, then his/her team wasn't going to take it seriously either.

There are other reasons why we have this rule. To begin, if the leader doesn't understand how the tool works, and doesn't understand their own traits, it will be nearly impossible for them to use this information accurately or effectively for anyone else. Think of it as starting by taking a good look in the mirror before you tell someone else how they look.

Your team will not appreciate being asked to complete a detailed assessment when or if they know that their boss has never done it. I've had clients who expressed a reluctance to ask their candidates or employees to complete an assessment because it can take over an hour to complete it, and they think they won't want to do it, or it will drive them away and make them look for opportunities at other companies.

I admit that I am a little 'old school' here, but my first answer to that potential scenario is, if they won't do something that you ask them to do that only takes about an hour before they come to work for you, what do you think they will refuse to do after they come to work for you?

And my second response when someone refuses to take the assessments is to explain, "If your boss thought it was worthy of his/her time to do this, then why do you think it is not worth your time to do the same?"

The first tenet of being a good leader is the revelation that it all starts with you. And this includes not asking people to do something you haven't done or are unwilling to do yourself. As my friend Brad Smith says, "Self-development begins with self-awareness".

Performance Improvement Begins with Selection

Once you understand how you are wired as the leader, it is time to start integrating assessments into the entire employee lifecycle in your company, and it normally starts with the selection process.

Most companies focus on two major areas when selecting new employees: what the candidate has done in the past, and how well they handle themselves in the interview process. Interviewing is another topic worthy of a book of its own, and I have met very few leaders who didn't think they were great interviewers (regardless of how many bad hires they had made in the past). To move forward, we will assume that you are at least competent in this area.

While both these areas are important to understand and evaluate for a potential new hire, their past and their interview skills don't tell you all you need to know to predict they will perform in the future in a specific role.

One of the consulting firms I worked for believed that if a candidate had been a successful *Account Manager* at one of our competitors, that they would likely be a successful *Account Manager* in our organization. Unfortunately, it rarely turned out that way. And mainly because we were missing a key ingredient in the selection process – which was the ability to compare the candidate to the top performers we already had in this role in our company.

One of the risks we must often address when clients start using *job match* information in the selection process is that they may start to put too *little* emphasis on these other two areas. I always remind them that these other two areas are still important parts of the selection process, and they shouldn't stop gathering and using this information, but they should also know how to leverage the job match information to maximize their hiring decisions.

A good place to start is to place equal weight on all three areas, so one-third of your hiring decision should be based on what they have

3-Part Selection Process

Past — Via Resume, Application, References

Skill Fit: Education, Training, Experience, Skills, Etc.

Company Fit: Attitudes, Values, Demeanor, Appearance, Integrity

Present — Via Interview

Most companies do this

Few companies do this

Future — Via Job Matching Tools

Job Match: Skills/Abilities, Personality, Interests

Your best chance at success is trying to replicate the *successful people already in your company*

done in the past, one-third of your decision based on the interview, and one-third of your decision based on how they compare to your top performers in this role. Said another way, if you aren't using job match information you are missing one-third of the critical information you could be using in the selection decision.

Now that we have covered the *theory* part of this discussion, now it's time to share some *actual results*.

CHAPTER 6

Predicting Future Performance (with Case Studies)

You might be wondering how we ever got started in this business, and the answer might surprise you. Shortly after I launched PeopleRight, I scheduled an appointment with a Regional Vice President of a Fortune 500 company. Notice that I didn't prospect the senior HR role, because the senior line Managers/Leaders are usually much closer to employee performance results than the HR professionals. We normally start working with senior Leaders to prove how our tools and processes can help them see how future candidates are likely to perform, and then work with HR roles later to integrate our tools and processes into the corporate HR procedures.

And truth be known, probably the only reason this first senior executive accepted my request for an appointment was that I had met him in college, and we had a lot of friends in common. In that first meeting, I asked him, "If I could help you solve your biggest people problem, would you hire me? After a polite laugh, he said, "Sure, if I thought you could help me solve it."

He was in an industry experiencing hyper-growth, and he shared with me that there were two key roles in his organization that were causing him the most problems, and if he could just find and keep more people who could perform in those roles his life would be much easier. I laid out a process where we could collect information to prove that we could help him find and keep more of these key players, and he agreed to let us try and prove it.

The basic process we have developed and perfected for working with our clients has three steps:

DEFINE   **ALIGN**   **REFINE**

Define means you tell us what is currently working for you.

The first step in predicting future performance is looking at the current performance of a team of people who are all performing the same role. You might imagine that the more people you have (i.e., more data you have) the more predictive the results will be, and you'd be right. You might think you don't have enough people performing the same role for the results to be predictive, so I will show you examples later in this chapter from roles where we had many different numbers of incumbents in the position.

It is always best to start with data from your own company, but in cases where you just don't have enough data, we can pull data from people in other companies who have been identified as strong performers in similar roles.

You might also think that you don't have any objective performance metrics or information on your current team, but even subjective ranking information can be useful. I've yet to meet a manager who couldn't identify who their best players were, and who their worst were.

Align means asking your current team to complete a whole-person assessment, and then combine their assessment results with the performance results to create high performer benchmarks. And depending on how much data is available, it could include using AI (i.e., machine learning) to maximize this benchmark.

Refine is adjusting your people processes to maximize the impact of collecting whole-person assessment results for both current and future employees and training all your hiring managers and people managers for this role how to best use this information.

As for the client I was describing above, after implementing this process for their first two key roles, the client was so impressed that he sent me the letter below:

D·R·HORTON DHI NYSE

May 2, 2003

Mr. Mike McCormack
PeopleRight
3748 Waldorf Dr
Dallas, TX 75229

Mr. McCormack,

Thank you for the outstanding service and support you are providing to my region. I am confident that your work is resulting in increased employee productivity and profitability. We started this partnership on a trial basis, and we were only looking at two roles in two offices. The initial goal was to determine whether or not we could improve the quality of our business results by improving the selection process for these roles.

Not only have we established confidence in your services in helping us improve our selection process for new employees, but in the coaching and development process for our existing employees as well. We have expanded their use beyond the original sales and construction management roles to the point where we have now used them in senior level accounting roles and in senior management roles in my organization.

After seeing the results thus far, in multiple roles and multiple locations across the entire region, I am now committed to using these tools across all 13 of my divisions across the Northeast U.S.

Thank you for the presentation you made to the Sales Managers in April. They have all committed to additional use of the assessment in order to continue to improve their business.

Sincerely,
D R Horton, Inc.

George Seagraves
President Northeast Region

And the rest of the story is: …it worked…and we have built benchmarks for over 100 other roles for this company now, and we are still working with them today, over 20 years later!

Next, we will share actual case studies showing the results our clients have achieved.

Case Study 1:

Position: Loan Officer

Number on team: 6

Performance criteria: Subjective (Manager ranked them 1 to 6, and believed that he had 3 A-Players, 3 B-Players, and no C-Players). The manager also shared objective metrics of how many loans each loan officer closed, but we only used the manager's ranking information to decide who we would include in the benchmark.

Process: We used the assessment results from the three A-Players to create a benchmark showing what they had in common across 20 traits in three major categories (cognitive, behavioral, and interests), then compared all six loan officers to this benchmark.

A summary of the results is below:

- The highest ranked Loan Officer had the highest overall job match
- The lowest ranked Loan Officer had the lowest overall job match
- The average **overall job match** for the three highest ranked Loan Officers was 10 points higher than the average **overall job match** of the three lowest ranked Loan Officers
- The *cognitive job match* was 12 points higher for the higher group versus the lower group

- The ***behavioral job match*** was 12 points higher for the higher ranked group versus the lower ranked group

First Name	Pattern Name	Overall - % Match	Cognitive - % Match	Interest - % Match	Behavioral - % Match	Ranking (1 to 6)	FY Loans completed
Rank 1	Loan Officer	93	95	87	95	1	191
Rank 2	Loan Officer	92	93	84	95	2	182
Rank 3	Loan Officer	90	95	76	92	3	137
		92	94	82	94		170
Rank 4	Loan Officer	84	93	75	79	4	40
Rank 5	Loan Officer	81	68	87	92	5	138
Rank 6	Loan Officer	81	86	81	75	6	98
		82	82	81	82		92

Top three averaged 78 more loans closed than Bottom 3!

Using their performance data with our results we calculated the ROI for this study.

- Top performers completed 78 more loans per year than bottom performers
- Average profit/completed loan was $1,500
- If they used this information to select and hire just one more top performer in the future (vs. a B-performer) the <u>increased annual profit</u> would be $117,000
- Cost of this study was $5,000 (including the assessment costs to cover the next 3 candidates)
- ***($117,000 – $5,000) / $5,000 = 2,240% ROI***

Case Study 2:

Position: Sales

Number on team: 11

Performance criteria: Subjective (Manager ranked them 1 to 11, and believed that he had 5 A-Players, 6 B-Players, and no C-Players). The manager also shared objective metrics of how many deals each salesperson closed, but we only used their ranking information to decide who we would include in the benchmark.

Process: We used the assessment results from the five A-Players to create a benchmark showing what they had in common across 20 traits in three major categories (cognitive, behavioral, and interests), then compared all 11 Salespeople to this benchmark.

A summary of the results is below:

- The highest ranked Salesperson had the highest overall job match
- The average overall job match for the five highest ranked Salespeople was 6 points higher than the average **overall job match** of the six lowest ranked Salespeople
- The **cognitive job match** was 5 points higher for the higher group versus the lower group
- The **behavioral job match** was 12 points higher for the higher ranked group versus the lower ranked group

Mgr. Ranking		Overall Job Match	Cognitive % Match	Interests % Match	Behavioral % Match	FY Units Sold	Units Sold/Month
1	Sales 1	95	95	95	95	56	4.67
1	Sales 2	87	95	73	86	44.5	3.71
3	Sales 3	86	79	93	89	44	3.67
4	Sales 4	83	86	73	84	64	5.33
5	Sales 5	80	86	68	80	68.5	5.71
Avg. Top 5 Performers		86	88	80	87	55.4	4.62
6	Sales 6	83	95	95	64	29	2.42
7	Sales 7	90	95	69	95	63.5	5.29
8	Sales 8	78	79	76	79	27	2.25
9	Sales 9	64	72	65	55	10	0.83
10	Sales 10	74	66	84	77	33	2.75
11	Sales 11	89	93	93	82	10	0.83
Avg. Lower 6 Performers		80	83	80	75	28.75	2.40

Top five averaged 27 more units/yr. than Bottom six!

Using their performance data with our results we calculated the ROI for this study.

- Top performers sold 26 more units per year than middle performers
- Average profit/completed unit was $24,000
- Using these job match numbers we could have predicted 80% of their top performers and 50% of their middle performers *before* they hired them
- If they used this information to select and hire just one more top performer in the future the <u>*increased annual profit*</u> would be $624,000
- Cost of this study was $10,000 (including the assessment costs to cover the next 10 candidates)
- *(($624,000 X .8 X .5) − $10,000) / $10,000 = 2,396% ROI*

Case Study 3:

Position: Sales

Number on team: 23

Performance criteria: Combined – Manager ranked his team 1 – 23 and provided objective sales information for previous 12-month period. We combined this information, placing 50% weight on each criterion (rank and units sold) to come up with a *Combined Performance Score*. We then used regression analysis with the *Combined Performance Scores* to determine Top and Bottom Performers. (Top performers were those who scored one standard deviation above the mean score, and Bottom Performers were those who scored one standard deviation below the mean score).

Process: After the regression analysis we had 5 Top Performers, 13 Middle Performers, and 5 Bottom Performers, and we used the assessment results of the 5 Top Performers to create the benchmark, then compared all 23 Salespeople to this benchmark and compared the average scores of Top, Middle, and Bottom Performers.

A summary of the results is below:

- The **Top Performers** all scored at least 85% overall job match, and the average was 89%
- The **Middle Performers** average overall job match was 78%
- The **Bottom Performers** average overall job match was 72%
- The **Top Performers** closed 22 deals/year, the **Middle Performers** closed 14/year, and the **Bottom Performers** closed less than 8/year.

Predicting Future Performance (with Case Studies) 47

First Name Last Name	Mgr. Rank	Overall Job Match	Combined Performance Score	Net Sales Units	Units/month
Top Performers	1	85	1.892	22.00	1.83
	2	91	1.786	21.00	1.75
	5	93	1.643	23.00	1.92
	1	91	1.642	16.50	1.38
	6	85	1.607	29.00	2.42
		89		22.3	1.9
Middle Performers	9	74	1.464	29.00	2.42
	6	88	1.321	18.00	1.50
	3	88	1.286	12.50	1.04
	3	83	1.143	10.00	0.83
	12	75	1.071	20.00	1.67
	2	77	1.071	8.00	0.67
	11	66	1.036	18.00	1.50
	8	84	0.893	11.00	0.92
	15	90	0.858	19.00	1.58
	4	64	0.786	4.00	0.33
	12	73	0.75	13.00	1.08
	13	71	0.715	15.00	1.25
	11	83	0.572	9.00	0.75
		78		14.3	1.2
Bottom Performers	10	64	0.5	7.00	0.58
	10	77	0.5	7.00	0.58
	13	61	0.357	8.00	0.67
	18	73	0.285	10.00	0.83
	14	84	0.178	6.00	0.50
		72		7.60	0.63

Using their performance data with our results we calculated the ROI for this study.

- **Top Performers** sold 8 more units per year than **Middle Performers**, and 14 more units than **Bottom Performers**
- Average profit/unit sold was $30,000
- If they used this information to select and hire just one more **Top Performer** in the future and avoided hiring a **Bottom Performer**, the _increased annual profit_ would be 14 units X $30,000 = $420,000
- Cost of this study was $15,000 (including the assessment costs to cover the next 6 candidates)
- *($420,000 - $15,000) / $15,000 = 2,700% ROI*

Case Study 4:

Position: Financial Services Professional

Number in the position: 68

Performance criteria: Objective: All 68 people in this role were measured using the same four key performance indicators (KPIs), which were all objectively measured. The leader of this role wanted to know if we could help them predict how successful new candidates were likely to be in this role, and if we could predict success across all four KPIs, because they were planning to hire 10 more people into this role in the coming year.

Process:
The manager of this role provided performance results for all 68 incumbents in this role, across all four KPIs in this role, for the previous 12-month period. All 68 incumbents completed a whole-person assessment measuring 20 different traits in three different categories: cognitive, behavioral (personality), and interests.

We combined the assessment results with the performance scores and then used regression analysis to determine the Top and Bottom Performers (i.e., those scoring one standard deviation above or below the mean performance score of the group). The results showed they had nine Top Performers, 52 Middle Performers, and 7 Bottom Performers.

We then took the assessment results of the Top Performer group and created a benchmark showing what they had in common, and since we had a sufficient amount of data, we engaged a data scientist to apply machine learning to produce hundreds of different (but similar) iterations of this model to see if we could increase the odds of predicting job success and came up with a maximized version of this benchmark.

Note: Engaging data scientists who can use AI (i.e., machine learning) to help refine these patterns is something very few consultants are doing with this type of information, and we have been doing it for over eight years (when the amount of data can support the additional analysis)! It gets back to my 'nerdy' engineering background. I understand the processes and the data analytics, and I have found some great resources who can integrate it all together and make it happen.

After creating and maximizing this benchmark, we compared all 68 incumbents to the benchmark, and a summary of the results is below:

- The (9) **Top Performers** average overall job match was 87.9%
- The (52) **Middle Performers** average overall job match was 80.3%
- The (7) **Bottom Performers** average overall job match was 77.3%
- *The benchmark accurately differentiated performance of **ALL** three performance groups across ALL 4 KPIs*

	# in Group	Touches/8 hours	Audit %	Error Rates	Avg. Touches per Month	Overall Job Match Avg.
Top Performers	9	8.4	1.75	0.37	203.6	87.9
Middle Performers	52	6.4	2.46	0.62	128.4	80.3
Bottom Performers	7	4.9	5.99	1.42	90.6	77.3

Top Performers scored better in ALL 4 KPIs than Middle Performers, and Middle Performers scored better in ALL 4 KPIs than the Bottom Performers.

But it gets even better in this case. After we saw that the benchmark was predictive across all four of the KPIs, our data scientist created a 'Scorecard' that the client could use when evaluating future candidates for this role. The scorecard enabled them to enter a candidate's raw scores from all 20 of the traits that were measured on the assessment, and then run an algorithm to predict whether this person was likely to become a Top, Middle, or Bottom performer.

When we ran the 68 incumbents' raw assessment scores through the scorecard, *it accurately predicted which group they would have*

ended up in 68 out of 68 times! Just think, if you had a tool that would predict whether someone would become a Top, Middle, or Bottom performer on your team, how much would that information be worth to you! And think of how you may have been able to avoid most, if not all, of the bad hires you have made! How much easier could *you* sleep at night!

And because of the large amount of data that we had; we could also share with the client which of the 20 traits were *most effective in predicting performance* results. We obviously can't guarantee that every time we have this much data that we can produce these kinds of stellar results, but we can confidently say that the more data we have the more compelling the results tend to be.

Using their performance data with our results we calculated the ROI for this study.

- ***Top Performers*** completed 80 more transactions/year than ***Bottom Performers***, and the average profit/transaction was $1,500

- Historically they had hired just as many ***Bottom Performers*** as ***Top Performers***, and they planned to hire 10 more people in this role in the coming year.

- If they use this information to hire 2 more ***Top Performers*** and avoid hiring 2 more ***Bottom Performers,*** they could close an additional 160 transactions/year.

- Cost of this study was $26,500 (including assessments for the next 10 candidates)

- 80 transactions X 2 people X $1,500 = $240,000

- **_($240,000 - $26,500) / $26,500 = 806% ROI_**

Big Takeaways

I mentioned earlier that I have an engineering degree and started my professional career as an engineer. And most engineers like to reverse-engineer things, especially things that work. This approach not only applies to recreating efficient machinery, but also to business processes and people. The three basic steps in reverse engineering are information extraction, modeling, and review.

I've just shown how we can collect information about how people are wired and how they are performing, combine this information and see what the best performers have in common, then use this information to accurately predict who will likely be successful in the future. ***Bazinga!!!***

What if you could predict who (among your candidate pool) will be successful BEFORE you hire them? For example, if you knew someone was likely to perform like your C-Players, would you still hire them?

How much would that kind of information be worth to you?

How much better would you sleep at night?

And how much more fun would your family vacations be!

For Those Who Are Still Skeptical

Some people might look at one or more of the case studies above and say, 'Yeah, but the difference in job match scores isn't that different among the different performance groups, so does it really work?'

Remember the McKinsey and Company 2023 study we referenced earlier that showed the highest performers in a role could be 800% more productive than average performers in the same role. Stop and think what the actual numbers are for your team. If a small difference in job match can result in an 800% performance difference, wouldn't it be worth at least a trial project to see if it works?

The thing to keep in mind is that even small improvements in your people decisions over time can result in huge differences in performance. In the book **_Same as Ever_**, by Morgan Housel (2023), one of the chapters talks about 'Overnight Tragedies and Long-term Miracles'.

One of the examples in that chapter states that death rates from heart disease in the U.S. declined by 70% from the 1950s to 2015. That means that 25 MILLION more people would have died over those 65 years than did. Yet the *annual average rate* of decline in heart disease mortality between 1950 and 2015 was (only) *1.4 percent* per year!

The case studies above show much larger differences in performance between top performer groups and all other groups. But what *IF* the numbers were much smaller? Even a small increase in employee performance over time (from collecting and leveraging better information on your people) can have a huge impact on performance over the long run.

But using assessments in your *selection* process is only the starting point, and we'll discuss the bigger picture next.

CHAPTER 7

Great Job Match Leads to Building Better Leaders

We have covered a lot of ground in this book, and the major focus has been on how to improve job match, and job match usually starts in the selection phase of the employee lifecycle. But when you step back and look at the bigger picture, it is only the beginning. I like to teach my clients to think about it as the entry level, or '*Level 100*' coursework towards the goal of becoming a great Leader.

The Employee Lifecycle

Creating Value for Clients
We support our clients through the full employee life-cycle, helping them identify the best people for their jobs and then developing them to their fullest potential.

Selecting — Developing — Developing Leaders
Level 300

| PRE-SCREENING | JOB MATCHING | ON-BOARDING | MANAGING PERFORMANCE | SUCCESSION PLANNING |

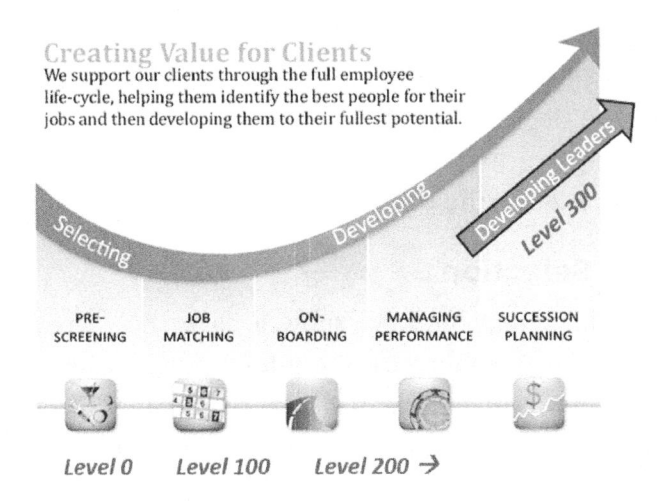

Level 0   Level 100   Level 200 →

Unfortunately, a lot of people *only* think of job match during the selection phase and forget about how important it can be to **ALL** the other phases of the employee lifecycle. As I've stated earlier in this book, I've tried to limit the content so that this could be an easy (i.e., short) read for most leaders.

The topics described in this chapter could be entire books (or genres) of their own, and there are hundreds (thousands?) of books that focus on Teambuilding, Managing Direct Reports, Communications, and Leadership Development. In this chapter I will stay focused on how mastering the art and science of job match can give you a serious head start on excelling in these other areas as well.

To say it another way, great job match makes onboarding, coaching, succession planning, and leadership development so much easier, and poor job match makes all these areas harder.

I like to use the college degree plan framework to expound on these topics:

>   *Level 100* – Improving job match for selection
>
>   *Level 200* – Using better job match to improve onboarding and performance management
>
>   *Level 300* – Understanding how job match can positively impact Leadership Development
>
>   *Level 400* – Mastering all these levels, while adding inputs from 360-degree Leadership toolsets.

Now, let's discuss these levels one at a time.

Level 100: Selection

You might think that once we show a client how predictive job match can be, they would trust the information and use it in ways that would improve the performance of their teams. Have you ever met someone who thought they were great at making selection decisions, despite what their hiring track record showed? Could you *BE* that person?

I once worked for a senior leader who thought he was a great judge of talent, and that he could decide whether to hire a person in the first five minutes of their interview. And he usually did (make up his mind in the first five minutes), and his hiring track record was about 50/50: half of them worked out and half of them didn't. But his confidence in his hiring decisions never wavered. He could have been equally successful if he had just flipped a coin!

I had another client who, *after* we had created a very predictive model for what performance looked like for his Sales team, would call me when he saw job match numbers that didn't look like those of his best people, and say things like, "I know this doesn't look like a good match, **BUT**... (and then he would tell me why he thought the candidate would still be a good fit for the role)".

I would always remind him of what the data had shown, and that I wasn't going to try to talk him out of hiring this person. Afterall, all I could see were the candidate's results compared to the high-performer benchmark, and he was looking at a lot more information about the candidate, including who they had worked for, how long, and had probably met with them at least once to see how they conducted themselves.

All I asked him to do was, **IF** he chose to hire this person (who did not look like a good fit), to call me back in two to six months and let me know how that hire turned out. And every time he chose to ignore what the job match showed, and hired the person anyway, he would call me back and admit, "Yeah, I should have trusted what the job match was telling us." After *ignoring* the job match scores three or four times and seeing how those situations turned out, he finally started trusting what the job match scores were telling him.

You also might think that once you know how to use this information you are ready to roll, but what about all the other managers in your organization who are involved in the selection process? Have they all completed the same assessment? Do they understand their scores? Have they seen and reviewed the high performer benchmarks that were created using the assessment results from your best employees? Have they been thoroughly trained in how to use this information in the selection process? One of the biggest advantages of working with PeopleRight is that we will make sure that all your hiring managers are trained in how to *effectively* use this information!

Level 200: Onboarding, Management Performance, and Succession Planning

When on-boarding new employees, the main goal is to get them oriented in the new job and get off to a great start as fast as possible. If the new hire is wired like your best performers are wired, then they will do a lot of things that your top performers do *naturally!* They don't have to operate outside their comfort zone to do the things needed to be successful in this job. But if they aren't wired like your best people are wired, then they will have to get out of their comfort zones to do what it takes to be successful.

Each time they must get outside their comfort zone to be successful you can think of it as you are putting them in stress mode. So, if they are a 'close' job match, it may just be a little bit of stress, but if it is a poor job match, it could be a lot of stress.

In addition to knowing how they compare to your best performers, and being able to coach them accordingly, you can also know how their traits compare to *yours*, and as a result, how you might best coach, manage, and lead them.

When someone on your current team is not performing up to the level they need to, and you have collected the information about how they are wired, you can look to see if the problem is that they just aren't wired like your top performers are wired. Or they may not be wired like most of the other people they are working with. Or they may be wired so differently from you that you need to consider other ways you might lead them to help them achieve higher performance.

Companies that have used our tools to create high performer benchmarks for multiple roles in their organizations can also use this information to aid in their succession planning activities. Think how powerful it would be if you could see not only how good a match someone is to their current role, but also how good of a match they are to a potential future role. Think about how useful this information could be in improving the career growth opportunities for your people. And remember, career growth is one of the top four categories of what your employees want the most.

We have one client that hires a lot of summer interns every year, and some of these interns stay in the same role all summer long, while others may move around into two to four different roles during the summer. After tracking this for a few years, we could see that there were three or four key roles that interns usually worked in, so we created a report showing the managers of these interns the job match scores for all these key roles. Now they can steer interns towards roles where they are a better fit and create an environment that is likely to be beneficial for both the interns (because they are doing work that they are naturally good at) and the company (because more stuff gets done)!

Level 300: Foundation for Leadership Development

I want to start by emphasizing that a tool focused on job match is not necessarily a great tool for leadership development, but it can be a great input for understanding some of the basic reasons *why* people are behaving as they are as leaders, and *how other people likely see them* as a leader. This includes how others see their traits as *strengths*, and how they might see their traits as *challenges*. I like how a colleague of mine, Tatyana St. Germaine, refers to this as using the tool to help them understand their 'Leadership DNA'.

Level 400: **Leadership Development**

Leadership development typically includes a 360-degree tool, i.e., one that lets others (boss, peers, and direct reports) rate the leader on how well they are leading in certain areas. It also includes a formal development or coaching program based on the feedback that the leader receives from the people around them, as well as a follow-up leadership assessment to see if they have improved in any of the areas that they chose to work on.

None of these other levels are beyond the scope of our company and the services that we can provide, but since I promised to keep it short, they are beyond the scope of this book. Much more could be said about all these different uses of the information, but I promised to keep this book short so it could be a quick read.

And as we are coming near the end, I want to share just a little more about where all of this is going.

CHAPTER 8

Moving Into the Future

We have already covered a lot of ground, and if you have stayed with us this far you know more about assessments and how they can predict job match and job performance than 99% of the leaders out there.

I hope that you have seen how using the right assessments and processes are not only beneficial to you as a leader, but they are also beneficial to your employees – because no one wants to work in a job where they are not a good fit or where they can't be a strong contributor.

You have read about, and likely have experienced, how different assessment instruments measure different individual traits, and some of those traits can be a lot more important than others, and the way that they are measured can have a huge impact on the results they might be able to deliver. And choosing the right partner to help you implement the processes needed to maximize job match to improve performance can also have a huge impact on the results.

And you have seen how our tools and procedures have helped our clients achieve some amazing results for over 20 years. But you might be thinking, or you *should be* thinking, 'Yeah, but how does all of this work moving forward into the world of AI and who knows what else?' While no one can know all the answers about what's coming next, you can be assured that there will be some companies on the leading edge of change to enhance employee productivity.

You may have noticed that I mentioned back in Case Study #4 the fact that we used AI (i.e., machine learning) to maximize this benchmark, and we did this back in 2016 when most people didn't even know what AI was! And we have continued to use this technology in cases where we had enough data to improve the predictability of our benchmarks.

And we are always looking for ways to leverage AI technology to provide world-class results for our clients. Just this year we started adding more analytic capability to show leaders how to get the best out of all their employees, and below I'll share an overview of a project currently underway.

The client came on board and started using our tools and processes in 2022, and after using them for two years they wanted to see how well their tools and processes were working to help them predict and improve their team's success, and if we could tweak the benchmark to be even more predictive. They shared performance results from two separate KPIs for their sales team and told us how much weight they wanted us to apply to each metric. In this case, they wanted us to put 80% weight on one of the metrics, and 20% weight on the other one.

The final data analysis is just wrapping up as I write this, but here is what we know so far:

- Since starting to use our tools and processes two years ago they have hired far fewer poor performers now than they did in the past
- The new benchmark that we created from top performers results are predictive for both of their key metrics, and they are predictive not only *Overall Job Match,* but also for all three of the sub-categories of information that we measure (abilities, personality, and interests)

But here is where the look to the future starts to kick in, and we are seeing some incredible things. Keep in mind that we objectively measure 20 different individual characteristics with our core toolset, and for this client we can take these results to a level they haven't seen before, including:

- For each one of the KPIs that they measure, we can show them the three most predictive traits (out of the 20) that drive performance the most
- We can also show them how much they might be able to improve performance (for each KPI) if they were to create individual coaching plans for each employee focusing on these three key traits
- So, no longer do they have to put everyone through the same training, because not all of them need the same things, and we can show them the areas where coaching can impact performance the most for everyone on their team and show them whether they should try to help the employee to exhibit more *or less* of these traits.

Remember back in chapter 3 when we shared what your employees want, and *career growth was one of the top four themes* that employees value the most. You don't get career growth without having effective professional development. Just stop and think what would happen if you could have a conversation with your employees that goes something like this:

Leader: "If I could share something with you that would help you do your job better, would you want me to share it?"

Employee: "Well, sure, why wouldn't I want that kind of information."

Leader: "Remember back when you started, and we asked you to complete an assessment that you probably thought was a little over the top in terms of all the things it asked you? Well, it turns out that one of the reasons we asked you to do this was that it measured 20 different traits, and we have found that there are certain traits that help people in your role perform better. While we are not asking you to be someone that you aren't, we can share that when people exhibit just a little bit more (*or less*) of this trait than you do, that they usually perform at a higher level."

Using this kind of approach, you have put professional development in the employee's sphere of control, and they can decide if they want to work on it or not. There is no guarantee that wanting to work on it will allow them to adjust their behaviors enough to cause a difference in performance, but it certainly gives them a great opportunity to do so.

Just stop and think about a time when you had to sit through some training that wasn't meant for you because you were already good or proficient in that area – but you had to go through it because *everybody* had to go through the same training. How insignificant did it make you feel? How much did you think of it as a waste of time? Did you ever think, *'I just wish they would pay me more money instead of making me sit through this training that I'm sure they are paying a ton of money for!'*?

In one of my past roles, I was responsible for training leaders in a consulting organization how to be better staff managers, and one of the hardest things to accomplish in that role was how to find training and/or development opportunities that would be worthwhile for everyone, without having to break into Fort Knox to pay for it. And no matter what we offered – it was never equally beneficial to all who had to sit through it – because they were all wired differently, and they all brought different strengths to the table.

I never worked for a company that had an unlimited professional development budget, and I bet you haven't either. Developmental budgets are always constrained, and they become even more constrained in tough economic times – so just think about how much more effectively you could use those resources for your team if you could focus only on the areas that you can link directly to improving their performance!

The future is already here, and it will continue to evolve through better tools, processes, and analytics (including more AI) – and you can be the leader who is not only a part of it, but on the leading edge.

In the last chapter we will wrap all this up with some ways to get started if you are ready to increase your team's performance.

CHAPTER 9

Afterwards: Taking the Next Step

We hope you have enjoyed this short book on the importance of job match, and how it positively affects almost everything related to job performance and the employee life cycle.

We trust you gained value from the contents of this book, and for those who are looking to apply any of what you have learned to improve the business performance of your team we offer three ways that our current clients used to get started:

> ***Crawl***: Reach out and ask to complete our whole-person assessment. We will schedule you for the assessment plus schedule a review session where we will review the results with you and show sample reports that can help not only in selection phase, but also used in all other phases of the employee lifecycle.
>
> ***Walk***: Have your entire Leadership Team complete the assessment, and schedule a session to review the results, see the various reporting options, and discuss how to get started in a key role in your organization.

Run: Call us to discuss how to collect information and build a benchmark for one or more key roles in your organization. We will include the other options listed above when we take off running.

If you would like to speak with the author about any of the options above, you can schedule an introductory ***Zoom*** call here:

If you prefer to use ***Teams*** instead of ***Zoom*** for our call, use the link above to find an open time on my calendar, then send a ***Teams*** invite to info@people-right.com (and be sure to include in the ***Teams*** invite what the call is about).

About the Author

Mike McCormack is the Founder of PeopleRight Consulting LLC. During the first 20 years of his career, Mike worked for five different companies and had ten different job titles. And out of those ten jobs, there were eight that he hoped he would never have to do again. He created PeopleRight to help companies get people into roles that fit how they were wired, so they could succeed by using their natural talents.

Mike has a civil engineering degree and MBA from Texas A&M University, and he uses his analytical and business skills and knowledge to help companies use objective information to get the right people into the right seats sooner.

Mike has worked with multiple Fortune 500 companies, and 98% of his clients have continued to work with PeopleRight after their first project was completed.

Mike has been married to Vicki for over 37 years, and they have two grown children who have launched successful careers of their own, and four grandchildren. Mike enjoys biking, fishing, golf, and snow skiing.

What PeopleRight clients have said:

"The success of our company is dependent on adding teammates who can excel in their job, and who fit well into the company culture that we have worked hard to create. We have partnered with PeopleRight for over 10 years to help us make people decisions that improve our company's bottom-line performance, and they have demonstrated an ability to show measurable results across all roles in the organization."

Randy Present, Chairman of the Board,
DHI Financial Services, (a D.R. Horton, INC. Division)

'Our assessment benchmarks are 'dead on' right now. We say they are expensive, but it is not expensive when you consider the millions of dollars it saves us every year by avoiding bad hires.'

Karen Klemcke, VP,
Regional Manager, DHI *Mortgage*

"I have literally hired thousands of Salespeople over the course of my career and used many different tools in the hiring process. The tools and processes that Symon now uses from PeopleRight work far better than anything else I have ever used for predicting the performance of Salespeople. We have seen when hiring new salespeople that using PeopleRight's tools and processes results in over $250,000 additional revenue per hire per year."

Charles Ansley,
President & CEO (Ret.), Symon Communications

"I spent many years as an HR Executive and now run my own HR outsourcing company. I have used a variety of assessments in the past. Working with Mike and his assessments has been a game-changer! It has changed the way I hire and coach new employees."

Karen LaCroix, Founder and President,
Superior HR

"We now conduct PeopleRight assessments on every level position from Admin to VP, before making our hiring decisions. Our experience has proven it is much wiser to spend a few hundred dollars up front (on the assessment and a follow-up discussion with Mike) *and to give credence to the results*, than to hire effectively blind without it. We can count at least two instances where hiring without a PeopleRight assessment has cost the company multiple tens of thousands of dollars."

Dennis Smith, CEO,
Computer Business Solutions, Inc.

Made in the USA
Monee, IL
04 October 2024